How to make an extra income at the recycling center

Stop Putting Your Money Out For Pick Up

Uan Williams

NEWS FLASH

The New York Times published an article, by Sarah Maslin Nir, on March 20, 2016 that brings to our attention how New York City Sanitation Department feels about the trash residents put on their curbs. The city agency argues that once the garbage goes on the curb it belongs to them. Recyclables generate cash. They are okay with residents picking up bottles but they don't want them to be too organized. As a result of that, depending on where you are located, try to collect the recyclables before they reach the curb. You will learn some strategies as you read.

If you are living in a city that doesn't mind you picking plastic bottles off the curb, by all means be as organized as you can. If you are living in a city like New York, be strategic. The tips you'll learn as you read can be applied to wherever you are in the world. You just have to do your due diligence.

TABLE OF CONTENTS

Why I Wrote This Book

Many people are struggling to make ends meet. I've learned that not everyone who gets out of bed Monday morning and shows up for work is happy with the cash that HR deposit to their accounts on a weekly or fortnight basis. Many of the individuals I observed in the workforce are faithful workers who show up for work early and leave late. They are the hardest workers. Your hard work ethics doesn't inspire HR to work harder than you do to increase the cash flow to your direct deposit account.

I've seen cases where hard workers take on excess workload and go above and beyond to make their managers happy and are on the brink of losing their houses. Some can't afford their rent; they have to share space with friends, and some have called their parents to unpack their cribs. To make matters even worse, many good employees devoted years of service and never received a raise in 5 – 10 years while the supervisors and managers gave them a pat on the shoulders and say keep up the good work, you are doing a good job. "The company pays me top dollar to keep people like you."

Such lovely compliments are heart-warming but don't pay your rent (or mortgage), your college tuition or give you enough cash to buy an extra pair of pants to wear to work. People are hurting. People are hurting to the point where their situations have carefully brushstroke a painting over their eyes that prevent them from seeing opportunities under their nostrils. Some people might have been looking for better or second jobs for months and haven't hit the jackpot as yet. Some might lack the motivation to go and sit in a classroom because they cannot afford to pay college tuition and don't want a loan. It has gotten so bad that I see a growing number of people begging for help on the train, the streets and pantries. If you work at a company that has a pantry, in most cases, you are not allowed to reap that benefit to supplement your income.

Here's another frightening experience, I knew a custodian who retired from work because he had done his due diligence. A week after retirement, he returned to his company to inquire about his pension. Brace yourself; he was not prepared to receive HR's word. HR unapologetically reported to him that he didn't make any contribution to his pension plan. The individual was so devastated by the news that a week later he died. I don't know the cause of death but it was alarming.

I said all of that to say there's hope. You don't have to die before you're ready. There are opportunities wherever you are. You don't have to sell your property to dig for gold in California or elsewhere. There's gold between your ears. You can do something small, extra, while you are working and looking for better. A supervisor once told me a Chinese proverb that says something to the effect that "you can ride the cow while you look for the horse." The extra work doesn't have to be anything fancy or sophisticated. It can be as simple as picking up pennies or better yet, plastic bottles. Yes, it might sound like a little idea but don't despise small beginnings. This approach might work for you as a supplement if you challenge yourself. Don't limit yourself. Your current salary might have place limits on your investing abilities, but don't place any on the opportunity that's before you. What's interesting is that, once you're open to an idea, more will take you over by surprise like receiving a deluge of rain after a long drought.

OVERVIEW

"Somebody's garbage is another person's treasure."

Everyone throws away trash but not everyone benefits from their waste. Based on my research I've discovered that every individual, in America, throws away at least three pounds of garbage each day. In addition to that, all of us drink water and in most cases, we purchased bottle water whether it is Poland Spring, Fiji, Nice, Big Win, Evamor, etc. Whatever the case might be we all contribute to generating garbage and all of us can benefit from our waste, not just a few groups. If you live in NYC, the city says your garbage is no longer yours the moment you put it out. If that's the case, do not put out your bottles for recycle.

Let's further put things into perspective, according to **KEEP AMERICA BEAUTIFUL, Inc.**, in 2001 the recycling industry generated over $236 billion in annual revenue. I always hear on the news that the economy is bad and people complaining about jobs and not making enough money while we are tossing it away daily. Yes, several industries are quiet, but I've never heard the recycling industry or the waste management industry complain about not having enough materials or better yet not enough waste. When you hear something in the media, it is usually, there is not enough space to dump your garbage or the regular complaints from your neighbors that sanitation didn't pick up their trash on time. So, there's always an opportunity available to generate some cash from this area as you put out your garbage on those specific days in your communities. The opportunity is within reach. It's in your pantry, kitchen, garage, car, streets, church, office, etc. You don't even have to look vigorously. It doesn't take much energy to look. Even in tough times it seemed like we consumed more and disposed of more. Also, KEEP AMERICA BEAUTIFUL also cited that with the increasing recycling rates, programs show that the industry is growing. What does that mean? It just means that they are more opportunities available to generate cash from our waste. The opportunity is here, and we cannot afford to let it slip away. It is a win-win situation for everyone including the sanitation department hence the government because it will help keep our streets much cleaner and boost the economy. This opportunity is within reach and it's called recycling your waste. This product is easy to find and easy to generate. It's a great way to supplement your income. It's also a great way to build a better relationship with your neighbors because you can make arrangements to dispose some of their garbage. You can assist them free of cost. You can help sort out their waste and take what you require. It will lessen their workload, cost them less time and money because they wouldn't have to purchase as much and use as much plastic bags they use on a weekly basis. As a result, you don't have to search the streets because I'm pretty sure your block has enough to get this project up and running. It has enough to generate your supply. The demand for plastic is there already. As time progresses and your relationship gets better you can have them put aside whatever waste you need to support your business. You can even set up a little area in your driveway or garage for your neighbor to drop off plastic bottles. If that doesn't work, you can have them give you a call to notify you ahead of time. As soon as they see plastic bottles, they think about you. As soon as recycling comes to mind, they think about you.

Since the discovery of plastic, the government has also discovered a problem because it's hard to get rid. Plastics are showing up all over on our beaches, rivers, springs, creeks, and streets. It's a problem that's unmanageable and bigger than us to handle. With that said let it be your goal to recycle every bit and while we're at it, make a few extra pennies. A penny earned is a penny saved. Now let's take a look at how our use of plastic has increased over the years. According to the INSTITUE OF SCRAP RECYCLING INDUSTRIES, INC. (ISRI), between 1950 and 2011 worldwide plastic production has grown annually by 9% and it has no intention of stopping. Also, global plastic production has increased by 10 million tons to reach 280 million tons. Now that's a lot of plastic, and that's a lot of financial rewards waiting for us to use to our advantage. You just have to cease the moment. We have the technology to recycle the plastics; we just have to get them to the plants. According to U.S. EPA, plastic recycling results in tremendous energy savings (an estimated 50-75 MBtus/ton of material recycled) compared with production of new plastic using the virgin material.

MINDSET

"Anyone can train to be a gladiator. What marks you out is having the mentality of a champion."
- Manu Bennett

If you have placed any limits on your thinking, remove them. It is not a get rich scheme or scam. It's simply an idea that you can immediately act upon to start reaping small rewards that add up over time like that savings jar you drop the coins in from your pocket daily after work. Don't see it as something degrading or beneath your ability. It's not your destination, but it has the potential to help get you there. Think of it as a means that will contribute to propelling your goals to arrive at an earlier date. Think of it as the jet stream that disrupts your thinking and what you have been settling on. Many people have started from much humbler beginnings and are now reaping the end results. Some of your friends might talk negatively about you and drop your company but don't feel bad. They weren't your real friends. It took this entrepreneurial idea you were about to embark on to expose their authenticity as a friend. Yeah, people may laugh at you but don't let that be a hindrance to this pedal that will move you forward. At the end of the day, they are not the one helping you with your bills. They are not the one paying your car note, you do! If there's any form of pride in your stride let it slide away from your mind like an avalanche unless it's the pride to fend for yourself. If you allow coworkers and colleagues to discourage you, maybe this venture is not for you. But if you are tenacious and have the audacity to go for it, you are in for a treat.

It's important to develop the correct mindset because this business is not for those in a hurry, but for those who are patient and willing to trust the process. I remember visiting a pantry and met a lady who stopped by after the hours of operation. I was the one who brought her to the pantry because of her story. She had been retired for many years and fell on hard times. She said her only daughter abandoned her and kept on ridiculing her for picking up bottles. Her daughter disrespected her but wasn't assisting her financially. So, this is only a reminder that when you become aware of an idea, you will face oppositions, but you have to wrap the concept into a seed and put it in fertile soil for it to germinate. Your mind is the ground for this idea to grow and blossom into that money tree that produces one dollar per day if you choose to. This idea is like the golden goose that lays an egg a day. You have to feed the goose for it to continue to bring forth eggs. So it is with this idea. You have to keep on encouraging yourself to get started and to endure. You can also try to associate yourself with similar individuals to serve as motivation.

WHAT CAN BE RECYCLED?

The focus of this book is centered on plastic drinking bottles even though they are several other types of plastic bottles that can be recycled among other items and other forms of plastic. If you live in New York City, you can call 3-1-1 or go to WWW.NYC.GOV/NYCRECYCLES for a comprehensive list of what can be recycled. That list will not tell you which item produces money, but it will give ideas to follow up on to see what waste product can put some "loose change" in your pockets. There are various types of plastic bottles. They come in different sizes, types and shapes. The way you determine if a bottle is recyclable doesn't require much work. You can look at the label that is wrapped around the containers. Next to the barcode you'll, usually, see 5¢ refund. Once that is present, you have no doubt that the bottle you have in your possession can be recycled. Once you see that 5¢ refund sign, you are in for a treat or better yet, you are in business. You've found your treasure. You've found gold, and you can call off the California gold rush. Usually, all of the major companies that sell drinking water in plastic bottles can be recycled. At check-out lines the supermarkets charged you a 5¢ refund fee in advance but how many times do you return the bottle to get your money? Maybe you haven't at all. Some of the major companies that sell drinking water are Poland Spring, Fiji Water, Dasani, etc.

Keep in mind that you can also recycle cans. Soft drinks are popular. You can find them from Pepsi, Coco-Cola, Dr. Pepper, Grace Coconut water, etc. Most of these cans are prevalent in developing countries in the Caribbean such as Jamaica, Haiti, etc. These are easy to find on the streets. Plastic will outlive some of us because they can withstand the test of time. Since that's the case, why not get some incentives from them. The manufacturers that produced containers and regulators guarantee us a 5¢ cash refund, and we are ignoring the opportunity. As you continue to read, you'll see where you can double the return for each cash refund per can.

PLASTIC BOTTLES

"Plastic recycling is bigger than the bin."
"Recycling a single plastic bottle conserves enough energy to light a
60-watt bulb up to six hours."

I'm selecting plastic bottles because they are the easiest to find. If you live in an urban city like NYC, you don't need to look far to find plastic bottles. As you step outside your door, bottles are everywhere. They are present from your steps to the subways. They are inside your kitchen, garage, and office. All you have to do is start to pick them up. Once you start looking for them, they will appear out of the blue. It's like buying a car, the moment you select the one you like that's when you start seeing them everywhere you turn on the streets. Guess what; the cars were always there. Aha, it's the same with plastic bottles, the moment you decide to look for them, they just start showing up everywhere. It's like the heavens just open up for you. You just have to be ready. When you purchase juice, water or liquid beverage from any store, just look at the package carefully. I know, usually, if it's plastic, it's recyclable. There might be some exceptions, so I recommend you look at the labels and all the packing for RECYCLE for the refund along with the 5¢ sign. Once that's present, you are ready to go. You are in for a treat. You are cooking with gas. At your place of work, you can start collecting them. You can collaborate with the custodial engineer and arrange for him to store them on the job for you. Depending on your agreement, you might have to pick them up daily, after you leave work, or at the end of the work week. Maybe the latter would be more convenient, but the main idea is that you have to arrange for pick up. If you have a vehicle, you can load them in bags and toss them in the trunk. Once you decide on how you are going to work with the custodial engineer, you can perhaps add to the pile from what you pick up during your lunch break.

On your fifteen or twenty-minute break, including lunchtime you can pick-up these plastic bottles and store them at your depot until you do the major pick up. You want to have a bag in your pocket, socks, knapsack or briefcase at all times. If you take the train daily, you can pick up these bottles and stash them in your bag. The subways are a great place to collect bottles since thousands upon thousands of people commute daily. You can also try to develop a relationship with workers in the subway for you to collect those bottles. If it's possible, you can even talk to the MTA and try to volunteer so you can collect as many bottles as you possibly can. The buses are a great place to look as well. Even though there is a sign that says do not litter, many people often ignore the sign for whatever reason. So, you could just take it that you are the reason why they left them there. Don't even bother to say how messy your fellow neighbors are, just thank them privately or publicly. You clean up after them. Their mess will help you play your game like chess. If you live close to where you work, that might be even better. It's better because you have at least two opportunities to pick up as many products as possible. On your way to and from work you can get as much as possible. I believe this would be easier for you because you don't have to make any arrangements with anyone. It's just you, your two hands and feet. Don't be surprised if you see drivers and passengers tossing bottles from out their car windows to the street. Don't take it as an insult. Just look at the brighter side, they are just trying to help you out. They are tossing out money into your bank account. Take it as if they are doing you a favor. It's okay. Nothing is wrong with that. You can walk your local streets and find bottles. You can even survey your local parks. Trust me anywhere people are, bottles are present by the loads. As you travel, the most important thing you want to do is to stay aware and alert. Once you are alert, you'll eventually begin to get ideas for more leads. You can even do a little research on the internet and look up major events like concerts, seminars, and marathons that are coming up in your neighborhoods or close by. A very popular event is barbecuing. People love to keep barbecues, especially on the major holidays like Labor Day, Independence Day, etc. Also look for fairs. That's another perfect place. When these events are in session, you can get there early and start collecting your products, or you can go to the venue just before it's over. After everyone leaves, that's when the major cleaning up work will begin. The vendors and other participants like event planners will personally thank you. Thank them as well because they might be tired and don't have the energy to do the extra clean up.

SIMPLY STRATEGY

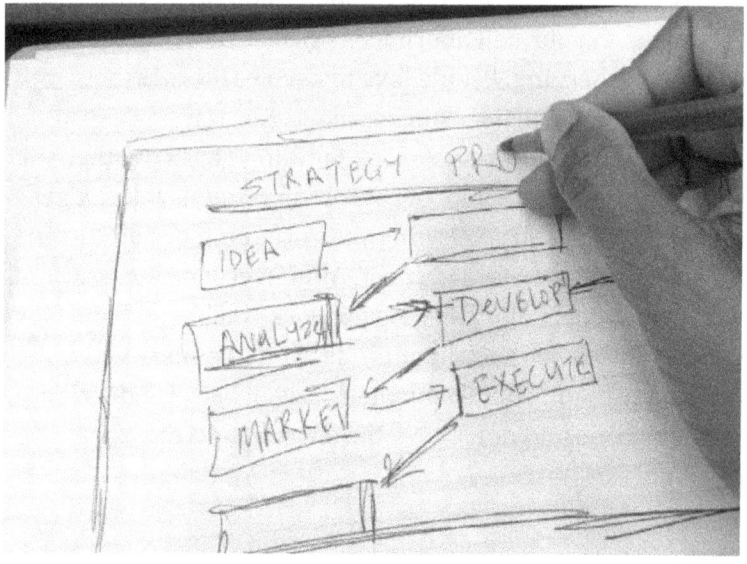

It is something I learned from someone who is active in this field. He has been doing this for more than three years. We have been friends for a while and one day I interviewed him and he revealed some remarkable stories and strategies. It felt like the heavens opened when he began to speak from his experience. From all the tips we talked about, here are the top three:

START SMALL

It is not a get rich machine or a scheme so it will require your due diligence. You will not become an overnight millionaire, but you'll be able to make an extra $100 - $200 on a weekly basis depending on how much time you invest. If you collect as little as twenty bottles in one week, that would be equivalent to $1. The bare minimum value you can sell one bottle for is 5¢. It is not difficult to gather twenty bottles for at least six days out of the week. A dollar a day is equivalent to seven a week, and you can do the math for the rest of the year. Please keep in mind that depending on where you sell your bottles, you can get anywhere from $0.05 - $0.13. You just have to negotiate your way for a better price than the suggested refund value listed on the bottle. The reason why I say negotiate is because after the drop off centers receive your bottles; they sell them for a higher price. It only makes sense for them to sell it for a higher price or else they would be unable to survive. According to Jim Rohn, "Profits are better than wages." The extra is what keeps them in business. I mentioned the prices just to give you a wiggle room to negotiate. So, if you should get 10¢ instead of 5¢ for each bottle, you will be able to get $2 per day for 20 bottles instead of 20 bottles for $1.

CREATE A ROAD MAP OF HOW YOU ARE GOING TO DO IT

When you create a roadmap, you are deciding on how much extra money you wish to bring in per day or week. You simply do what I did earlier by choosing to gather and sell twenty bottles per day. Once you get that out the way, decide on how long you will do that. After three months, you should be at least doubling what you have done in the initial stage. When you first got started, if you used to get a dollar a day, after three months you can say you want to pull in at least 3 dollars per day. After six months, you want to project how much money you want to gather per day or week. And hopefully, by a future date, you can project on how much money you should be getting from your extra activity. My friend also told me about someone he knows who got into the business for at least two years. At that time, he was able to retire from his day job and take on recycling full-time. He did so well that he had been achieving over $2000 per week and was able to open his facility, accumulate his pickup truck and hire a few employees. I am not saying this might be your faith, but if you so desire, it can work out for you after taking it small and remaining diligent.

DON'T GIVE UP

Whatever you do, do not give up. If you decide to quit, let it be after you accomplished your goals. Once you achieve your goals, and you choose to move on to something more rewarding, then you'll be able to take everything you've learned from recycling bottles and invest in your new endeavors.

DROP OFF CENTERS

Depending on where you live you might want to do a search on Google to get a list of the closest recycling centers in your area. The internet is filled with information. If you are in a remote area and don't have or have limited access to the web, you can stop by your local library or even look through a newspaper. If that doesn't work, ask someone. As a matter of fact, you can speak to sanitation workers about finding the closest drop off centers. I am certain you'll be able to get a lead. After you gather a list, you want to make a phone call to speak to someone there or better yet, go and visit the center. Once you visit the center, you'll get a better understanding of what they take and how everything works. After you gather a general understanding, you can make plans on how you're going to transport your products. I call it products because you are providing goods. Once you put a value on your products, it will change the way you speak and carry yourself. Remember, this is a business.

If you live in a big city like New York City you don't have enough hands to visit all the drop off centers. The good news is that any store that sells the recycling bottle you are looking to recycle will also buy it from you. The idea is that if they sell it, they will buy it. They will issue a refund. I learned that from Walgreens. I just so happen to be buying Fiji water daily until I saw a few bottles lying around the cashier area. One day I asked the clerk, "What are you doing with those empty plastic bottles?" "Oh we buy them from customers," she responded. I didn't know that. "So that means I can return these bottles along with other ones I bought and get a refund?" Her answer was yes, as long as it's a brand the store carries. After she had said that, a lightbulb went off in my head. I thought about all those water bottles I've bought and tossed in the garbage can. It became even more painful when she explained to me that most customers save up all the water bottles they purchased and just used the refund to buy a bottle of water to drink. I thought to myself, wait a minute, that's a brilliant idea. If you buy from Walgreens, Duane Reade and other supermarkets like Pathmark, they have a recycling area. Walgreens for example, allows you to drop them by the cashier while supermarkets such as Rite Aid have machines outside the store where you can drop off at your convenience without obstructing the flow of traffic inside the store.

Extra Benefits

The beauty of getting into the plastic bottle recycling industry is that you don't have to feel pressured or bullied to get involved. It is your choice. You get to decide your timetable on how early you want to get up or how late you wish to return home. The ball is in your court.

Every time I meet up with my friend, I noticed that he always has extra things for sale or things he found that are absolute keepers. For example, the last time I saw him he told me he had several items selling such as Xbox, PlayStation, new Apple headphones and MacBook Pro in exceptional condition. Each item he found has a story to go with them. The problem with the Xbox is that one of the buttons was a little hard to use. He put it on the market on sale for $60. The PlayStation only needed a good cleaning. The Apple headphones were only looking for someone ears. I ended up purchasing a pair from him for $20. There was only a small dent on the MacBook Pro that prevents the CD player from working. That is something that can easily be fixed for under $100. The Apple MacBook Pro laptop is valued just under $2000. He kept it for himself. When you decide to look for bottles, you not only get to learn about people. You get to learn about human habits and the psychology of how humans shop, use products, and react to products when there seems to be any form of glitch.

You get to learn about what's trendy as well as insights, and a few new tricks. Through my friends, I learned about the price of copper. He started collecting this metal from various electronic devices he bumped into on the streets and sold them to different buyers. Copper is becoming a very scarce commodity and instead of getting in the mining industry you simply get a bag, screwdriver, and you are in. There is no limit to what you can learn in the streets by weaving through people's garbage to find treasure. You are not digging through mountains of trash since, for example, in New York City, everyone usually separates their garbage from what's recyclable. That makes your task easier. The only thing is that after you remove your product, don't leave a mess. If you leave a mess, your neighbor will not be happy when you come around next time. A mess can be very costly for them. If you accidentally create a mess, tidy it because you don't want your neighbor to receive a ticket from the sanitation inspector.

Instead of allowing people to waste money and sanitation to reap all the benefit, why not get involve and help make your surroundings much cleaner.

SAFETY

Your safety is critical. I can't say enough about getting the proper gears to protect you from all sorts of bacteria. Since you will be picking up bottles from off the streets, your workplace, your neighbor's trash, crevices, corners, hallways, alleys, and other unforeseen places, you need to be equipped to protect yourself. I recommend that you wear a pair of gloves and carry extras just in case the ones you are wearing get damaged. I've seen people in masks so that might be a good investment. In addition to that, you want to walk with extra bags, and don't forget to dress in long clothing to protect your skin. If you decide only to save your bottles, you might not need to take the extra precautions as necessary. But you can't do enough to protect yourself. There's no such thing as over protection. I like the adage that says, "It's better to be safe than sorry." Also, if you are traveling with a shopping cart (or driving), you want to be on the lookout for traffic around you. Be careful about leaving your cart in the street. That presents a potential danger to others (such as pedestrians, cyclists, etc.) including yourself. If you are driving, you want to avoid double parking and leaving your vehicle unattended. Obey the traffic rules. As your business collections increase, I would suggest that you park your car legally and move around with a shopping cart if necessary. Make sure that when your bags are filled, you tie them securely to prevent accidents. Putting all the measures in place to avoid injuries to yourself and others is being a responsible citizen.

Conclusion

Recycling plastic is not a difficult task, and it doesn't require too much time. You can take advantage of the bottles you use in your home. Instead of putting them out for the sanitation department, set them aside for yourself and return them to the store for the extra pennies you were charged at check out. The stores charge a 5¢ upfront for the bottle and instead of following what most people do, which is toss out the bottles after use, you return the bottle for your refund. That's the least you can do. The store will get their extra pennies regardless of what you think because the price is factored in the total cost.

Plastic has become a big problem for our local and global communities so we might as well take advantage of this issue. The more plastic we recycle, the less litter and pollution we have to deal with on a daily basis. Plastic contributes to dirty beaches. We can curb this problem by doing our part as a responsible global citizen of the earth. Think about it, if you recycle, in this case, sell the empty bottle to the store, your environment would be much cleaner, and you will be at least 5¢ richer. The money the store took from you would return to your pockets to invest into something else. The stores automatically take the extra money from you so you might as well return the bottles to get what they took from you without your approval or permission.

Even if you don't have the time to return the bottles to the stores for a refund, you can save them for someone who will. You can easily find someone who is willing to take them to the warehouse, you don't have to look hard or do any research. Here's how simple it is to find someone. Whenever there's recycling day, the day you put out plastic for recycling, you'll see individuals walking around collecting these items the moment you start to put them out. Whenever you see these people, you can just give it to them. That would be your form of helping out.

REFERENCES

http://www.isri.org/recycling-industry/commodities-

specifications/plastics#.Vc_1hmTF-WY

Recycling Facts & Statistics - Keep America Beautiful

https://www.kab.org/

http://www.nytimes.com/2016/03/21/nyregion/new-york-

city-fights-scavengers-over-a-treasure-trash.html?_r=0

Image: Dreamstime.com